I0233937

A LITTLE TAX

By: J. Mobley

Illustrated by:
Indalecio R. Chavez Jr.

This book belongs to:

_____

A Little Tax

Copyright © 2021 Johnnie Mobley Jr.

ISBN: 978-0-578-88600-8

All rights reserved
No part of this book may be reproduced, or stored in a retrieval system,
or transmitted in any form or by any means, electronic, mechanical,
photocopying, recording, or otherwise, without express written
permission of the publisher.

www.alittleaccounting.com

Little J worked hard
for a small company,
but when he looked at his paycheck,
it was missing some money.

"Where is the rest?" said Little J,
before heading home to relax.
The payer said, "Don't worry,
I paid your government tax."

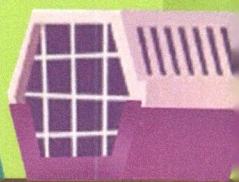

"A tax, a tax?
What is a tax?"
He wanted to know,
so he researched the facts.

PUBLIC LIBRARY

RESEARCH

CHECKOUT

Little J read a lot of books on taxes
and he learned super quick.
He even wrote down notes,
so that he could understand it.

"I think I got it!
It's quite clear to me,
taxes are how the government
gets its money."

The government uses taxes
to build things that Little J liked;
such as fire stations, libraries
and streets where he can
ride his bike.

Taxes can be good;
the more you give,
the more services people can get.
But! No one wants all
the money they earn
to disappear from their paycheck.

So there must be a balance,
to keep things fair;
those who earn the most,
pay a bigger share.

Once a year we file our taxes,
which means we send by mail,
a count of all the money we earned,
from working or what we sell.

If we need to pay more in taxes
we send the government a check,
and if we paid too much already
the government sends money back.

Tax Filing Plan

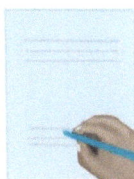

Now with all this info
all scattered about,
Little J was ready to file his taxes
and figure them out.

He gathered all the forms
and every receipt,
then organized his taxes
to make them quite neat.

When Little J filled out his tax forms,
he quickly saw,
that he paid too much in taxes
and was owed money back,
a big refund by law.

He sent in his tax forms
by April 15th,

and ...

His money came back,
after a couple of weeks.

Little J was happy,
with a refund check in hand,
because taxes were now in topic,
that he could understand.

Johnnie Mobley Jr., MBA, CPA, PMP

Author J. Mobley (Johnnie Mobley Jr.) is an accountant, consultant and professor. He holds degrees from Pepperdine University and the University of Washington. He has worked in accounting and finance with Fortune 500 companies, small businesses and governmental organizations. He writes books to help others by promoting financial literacy and business efficiency.

J. Mobley uses rhyme and visual examples to explain financial concepts. He speaks to kids and community organizations to promote understanding of finance and money. When he isn't working, he can be found with his family.

J. Mobley published his first book, "A Little Accounting" in 2019 which was met with immediate success, selling in multiple countries around the world.

Products and more info can be found online at:
www.alittleaccounting.com

Follow us on Twitter
@Accounting4kids

www.ingramcontent.com/pod-product-compliance
Lightning Source LLC
LaVergne TN
LVHW010027070426
835510LV00001B/21